T0042629

habitats

and the animals who live in them

habitats

and the animals who live in them

Anita Ganeri and Penny Arlon

weldonowen

weldon**owen**

Authors: Anita Ganeri and Penny Arlon

Design: Tory Gordon-Harris, Natalie Schmidt, Anna Pond

Editorial: Lydia Halliday, Susie Rae

Fact checker: Tom Jackson

Art Director: Stuart Smith

Publisher: Sue Grabham

Insight Editions Publisher: Raoul Goff

All photographs in this book including those used on the cover are used under licence from Shutterstock.com with the following exceptions:
Page 10, "Crab" © chiravan39/iStock
Page 36, "Pygmy Blue Whale" © Franco Banfi/naturepl.com

Copyright © Weldon Owen International, L.P. 2021

All rights reserved. No part of this publication may be reproduced, distributed, or transmitted in any form or by any means, including photocopying, recording, or other electronic or mechanical methods, without the prior written permission of the publisher, except in the case of brief quotations embodied in critical reviews and certain other noncommercial uses permitted by copyright law.

Published by Weldon Owen Children's Books

An imprint of Weldon Owen International, L.P.

A subsidiary of Insight International, L.P.

PO Box 3088
San Rafael, CA 94912

www.insighteditions.com

ISBN: 978-1-68188-742-5

Manufactured in China

First printed 2020

24 23 22 21 20 1 2 3 4 5

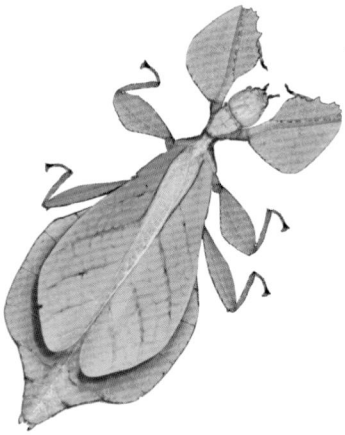

Contents

Beach	8
Mountain	16
Rainforest	24
Ocean	34
Polar	42
Desert	54
Grassland	62
Rivers and lakes	70
Woodland	78
Reefs	86
Urban	94
Camouflage	104

Look for the fun activities in each chapter. There are mazes, dot to dots, word searches, sticker scenes, and more!

Find the giant poster and sticker sheets at the end of the book!

Hello Habitats

From the highest mountains to the deepest parts of the sea, animals live all over the world. You can find them in scorching deserts, steamy rainforests, rushing rivers, and even at the icy ends of the Earth. The places that animals live in, and that provide them with food and shelter, are called habitats, and there are many different types. Some are hot and dry; others are cold and wet. Some teem with trees and plants; others are barren and bare. Habitats can be very large, such as an ocean or grasslands, or on a much smaller scale, such as a rock pool, or a single leaf on a tree.

Animals often have to adapt or change so that they can survive in their particular habitat. They have special features to help them. Animals that live in the sea often have bodies that are streamlined for swimming, and may also have flippers or fins. Animals that live in deserts are adapted to survive in the heat, and have special ways of finding water, even when it doesn't rain for weeks on end. Thick fur, feathers, or fat help animals at the icy poles to stay warm. Many animals are suited to life in one place, and may not be able to live in any other habitat or survive if their habitat changes.

In this book, you will meet animals from many different habitats, from wonderfully colored fish on a coral reef, to great herds of zebra and wildebeest roaming the grasslands. See if you can work out how they are adapted to life in their particular home.

Beach

A beach is an ever-changing habitat where land and sea meet. Beaches can be sandy or rocky, creating plenty of space for animals and birds to live and feed. But they are also challenging places to live in. They change shape constantly as the waves and wind wear them away, and, twice a day, the sea rises and falls on the beach, as the tides go in and out. Shoreline creatures must find ways of coping with being soaked by sea water, then being left high and dry.

Tern
Sea snail
Lobster
Seagull
Pelican
Cormorant
Parakeet
Ticks
Land snail
Kelp fly
Crawfish
Baby sea turtle
Spider crab
Whelk
Sand dollar
Puffin
Curlew
Clams
Sea lion
Sandpiper
Humboldt penguins
Scallops
Snow plovers

Anenome
Shore crab
Jellyfish
Blue swimmer crab
Sea stars
Abalone
Conch
Shrimp
Sea urchin
Limpets
Caiman
Lugworm
Swan mussel
Brittle star
Hermit crab
Sand hopper
Red land crab
Iguana
Goose barnacles
Rockskipper fish

Atlantic horseshoe crab
Sea anemone
Sea snail
Jellyfish
Ark clams
Sea louse
Killdeer
Dalmatian pelican
Siamese crocodile
Mosquito
Shore crab
Little ringed plover
Crayfish
Short-tailed shearwatert
Saltwater crocodile
Blue-footed booby
Crab
Mussels
Blue soldier crabs
Sea slug
Cockles
Limpet shells
Clams
Sea urchins
Kellen's whelk

Sea stars
Fairy penguin
Portuguese Man O War
Sea urchin
Razor Clams
Abalones
Marine crab
Flamingo tongue snail
Pied cormorant
Common Tern
Atlantic puffin
Nautilus
European sanderling
European cormorant
Oysters
Winkles
Whelk
Ghost crab
Great cormorant
American oystercatcher
Zebra mussel
Lobster
Seagull
Eurasian oystercatcher
Barnacles

On the beach

Head to the the beach to solve these puzzles. What will you find hiding in the sand and swimming in the rock pools?

Find the chicks

Follow the lines to help the birds find their chicks.

SHELL HOME

The hermit crab is born without a shell. It climbs inside an old shell left by another animal!

Maze

The baby turtle needs to find its way to the sea. Can you help?

start

finish

Word search

Find the beach creatures hidden in the word grid.

c	r	a	b	s
l	m	o	p	h
a	d	f	v	e
m	g	u	l	l
s	n	a	i	l

Gull

Crab

Clam

Snail

Shell

Mountains

With soaring slopes and snow-capped peaks, mountains can be perilous places. The higher you go, the colder and windier it gets and the thinner the air, making it harder to breathe. The slopes are sometimes bare and rocky; sometimes icy or covered in snow. Despite these harsh conditions, many animals make their homes on mountains. They soar and glide on the thermal winds rising above the peaks, clamber and climb up the rocky slopes, and take shelter in warm, underground burrows to avoid the worst of the winter time.

Takin
Muskrat
Goral
Black bear
Marmot
Ants
Alpacas
Japanese snow monkey
American bald eagle
Mountain wolf snake
Ribbed pine borer beetle
Mountain ringlet butterfly
Hercules beetle
Cougar
Dragonfly
Giant panda cub
Mosquito
Snowy plover
Red panda
Mountain nyala
Monal pheasant

Gray wolf
Cicada
Chamois
Honeybees
Pill bugs
Wild goat
Trout
Ticks
Mandrill
Andean cock-of-the-rock
Centipede
American beaver
Alpine chough
Bullseye giant silk moth butterfly
Tibetan Macaque
Boreal owl
Giant anteater
Ibex
Simien wolf
Snowcock

Snow leopard
Barbary sheep
Western diamondback rattlesnake
Andean condor
Yellow jacket wasp
Coyote
Apollo butterfly
Common raven
Longhorn beetle
Grasshopper
Reindeer
Moose
Llama
Monarch butterflies
Spectacled bear
Mountain kingsnake
Bhutan glory
Lynx
Walia ibex

Wild yak
Black widow spider
Rosy boa
Salmon
Pika
Painted lady butterfly
White-tailed deer
Golden orb spider
Mountain hare
Brown bear
Toucan
Markhor
Gorilla
Kea
Gelada baboon
Mouflon

Up the mountain

Wrap up warm to climb the snow-peaked mountain. Can you spot any animals with super-furry coats?

Sticker scene

Look for the eagles on your sticker sheet. Add them to the mountain scene.

Use your stickers here!

A WARM COAT

The yak has such long hair that it almost reaches the ground! It keeps the yak super-warm during the freezing winter.

Matching pair

Can you find two llamas that are exactly the same?

What comes next?

Look at the animal patterns. Can you work out which mountain animal comes next on each line?

Use your stickers here!

Rainforest

A thick blanket of lush, green forest grows around the steamy equator, which is the rainforests of our world. It is hot, wet and humid all year round in the rainforest, providing ideal conditions for animals to live in, with plenty of food to eat and places for breeding and shelter. In fact, rainforests are home to millions of plants and animals—more than anywhere else on Earth. They live in every layer of the forest, from the towering tops of the tallest trees, to the dark and gloom of the forest floor.

Fer-de-lance
Great hornbill
Tree kangaroo
Tiger beetle
Piranha
Jaguar
Resplendent quetzal
Spectacled owl
Giant anteater
Red-eyed tree frog
Tamandua
Leafcutter ants
Poison arrow frog
Orangutan
Sugar glider
Macaw
Okapi
Lowland gorilla

Sloth
Tailless whip spider/scorpion
Iguana
Civit
Howler monkey
Morpho butterfly
Jewel beetle
Sunbird
Oropendolas
Mandrill
Amazon kingfisher
Capybara
Fishing spider
Forest elephant
Tarsier monkey
Baby black caiman
Red ibis
Jumping spider
Toucan
Harpy Eagle
Yellow-headed caracara
Tapir

Anaconda
Nine-banded armadillo
Australian king parrot
Mosquito
Bat
Capuchin monkey
Ulysses butterfly
Scarlet macaw
Tiger
Blue and gold macaw
Gibbon
Common tree shrew
Cairns birdwing
Scorpion
Leopard
Stag beetle
Click beetle
Lemur
Hyacinth macaw
Ticks

Jaguarundi
Emerald tree boa constrictor
Spider monkey
Army ant
Buffon's macaw
Coati
King vulture
Binturong
Rhino beetle
Ocelot
Pangolin
Javan rhinoceros
Amazon parrot
Black panther
Jabiru stork
Heliconius
Tarantula
Chimpanzee
Giant rainforest mantis
Green-winged macaw
Loris
Longhorn beetle

In the rainforest

Hike through the rainforest to solve these puzzles. The rainforest is filled with animals, but they are sometimes hard to find!

Can you find?

Can you find two frogs, three spiders, four butterflies, and five ants?

FOREST GARDENER

Forest elephants are very important to the rainforest. They eat lots of fruit, spreading the seeds in their poop so that the seeds grow into new trees!

Odd one out

Which red-eyed tree frog does not have a matching twin?

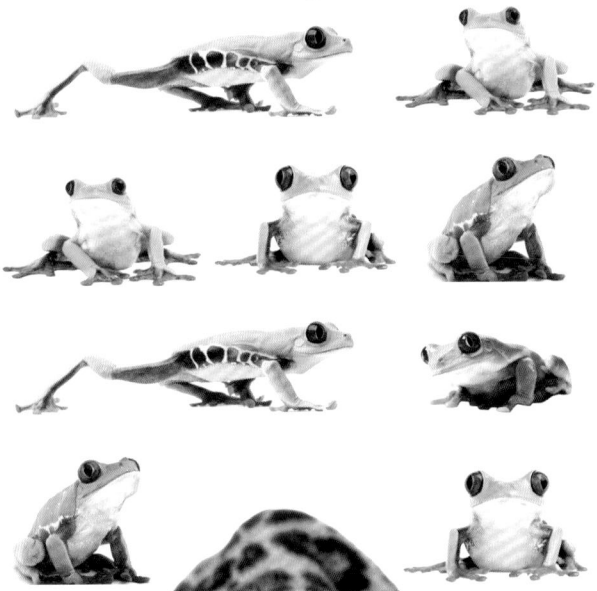

Color me in

Rainforest birds can be super-bright! Use lots of different colors for this parrot.

Anaconda

Monkey

Armadillo

Capybara

Shadow search

The jaguar is searching for its dinner. Look at the shadow! Which animal has it found?

Tapir

Follow the lines

Which frog will catch the cricket? Follow the lines to find out.

SPEEDY SWINGER

The spider monkey is the king of the swingers. It moves from tree to tree swinging by its hands, feet, and tail!

Draw the other half

Can you draw the other half of the rainforest beetles?

Odd one out

There are six toucans flying over the rainforest. Which one doesn't match the others?

Ocean

Vast stretches of salty sea water cover around two thirds of the Earth. This lies in five oceans—the Pacific, Atlantic, Indian, Southern, and Arctic. Together, they form the largest habitat on Earth. As you descend into the oceans, there are many different zones of life, from the vast expanses of the open ocean, to the freezing, blackness of the deep. These zones are home to a huge variety of animals, from microscopic zooplankton to gigantic blue whales, the largest animals that have ever lived.

Baby harp seal
Lobster
Scallop
Clymene dolphin
Skate
Giant triton
Hammerhead shark
Pygmy blue whale
Banded sea krait
Queen conch
Barracuda
Humpback whale
Ribbon eel
Stonefish
Atlantic cod
Sea lion
Goby
Electric eel
Flamingo tongue snail
Guitarfish
Shrimp
Hawksbill turtle
Crayfish

Manta ray
Whale shark
Longfin spotted snake
Sea lion
Jellyfish
Flying fish
Nautilus
Sea slug
Scampi
Bonnethead shark
Portuguese Man O War
Marbled stingray
Squid
Sailfish

Pufferfish
Flounder
Long-spine porcupinefish
Tiger shrimp
Blacktip reef shark
Blue-ringed octopus
Bottlenose dolphins
Seahorse
Dolphinfish
Beluga whale
Albacore tuna
Grouper
Bigeye fish
John dory
Moray eel
Walrus
Leafy sea dragon
Basking shark
Beluga sturgeon
Orca
Wolffish
Salmon
Trumpetfish

Narwhal
Bluefin tuna
Sardines
Moray eel
Blue marlin
Manatee
Red hump fish
Hermit crab
Deep-sea angler fish
Krill
Octopus
Red snapper
Squid
Manta ray
Green turtle
Honeycomb moray eel
Gray reef shark
Geoduck clam
Dugong

Under the ocean

It's a big, big ocean out there. Take a deep breath and dive into these watery puzzles!

How many left?

The hungry sharks are racing toward the fish. Will they get one each?

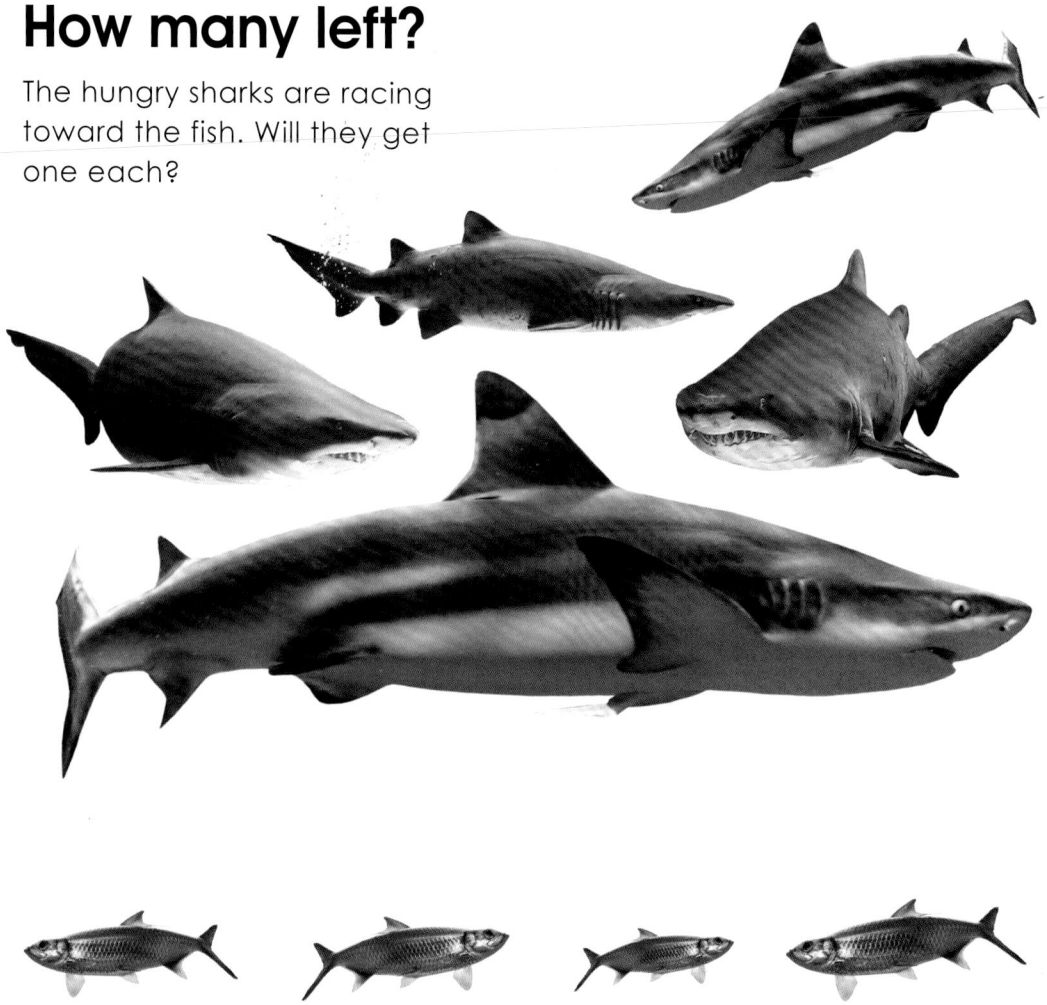

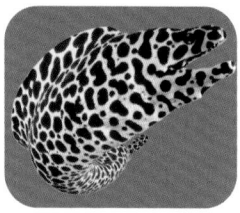

PLAYTIME!

Dolphins love to play with each other. They squeak and whistle, leap out of the water, and butt heads!

Sticker scene

How many sea lions can you find on your sticker sheet? Fill the kelp forest with sea lions!

Use your stickers here!

Odd one out

Look closely at the seahorses. Which one doesn't have a curly tail?

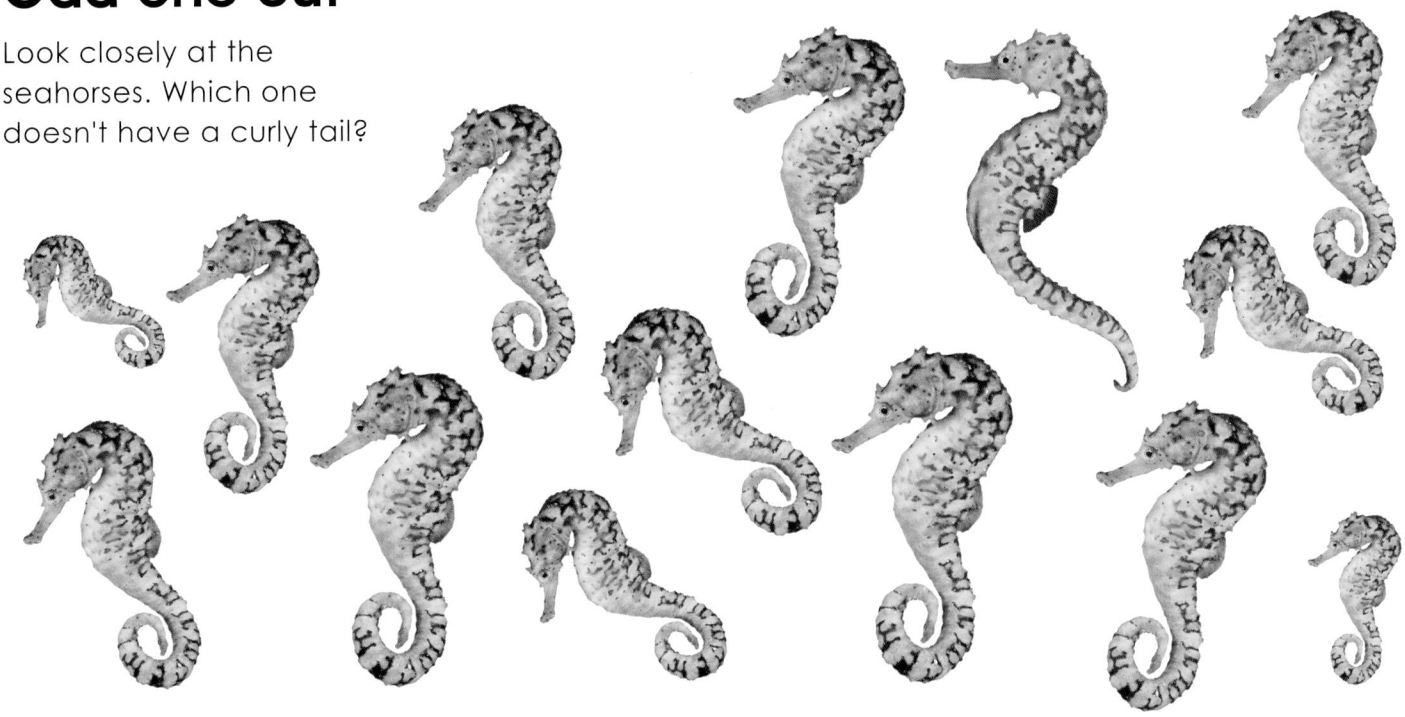

Polar

At the furthest ends of the Earth lie the coldest places on our planet—the Arctic and Antarctic, also known as the Poles. Here, it is always freezing cold and windy, and ice covers large parts of the land and sea. Polar animals are experts at survival. Polar bears, which are only found in the Arctic, have thick fur coats to keep them warm, and hairy feet that grip the slippery ice. Penguins, which are only found in the Antarctic, have thick, waterproof feathers that keep them warm and dry as they swim. In the icy ocean, some fish have chemicals in their blood that stop their bodies from freezing solid. In this section, we look firstly at animals that live in the Arctic, followed by those in Antarctica.

Arctic

Orca whale
Cod
Skua
Vole
Narwhal
Ground shrew
Lynx
Viviparous lizard
Gyrfalcon
Caribou
Arctic ground squirrel
Moor frog
Baby harp seal
Great gray owl
Arctic fox
Moose
Bald eagle
Marmot
Walrus

Woolly bear caterpillar
Lemming
Beluga whale
Dall sheep
Damselfly
Wood frog
Arctic tern
Polar bear
Siberian husky
Canada goose
Snowy owl
Arctic hare
Arctic char
Bearded seal
Ptarmigan
Musk ox
Red fox
Snow goose
Wolverine
Puffin
Arctic wolf
Barnacle goose
Roe deer

Antarctic

Krill
King penguins
Albatross
Gentoo penguin
Crabeater seal
Adelie Penguin
Antarctic petrel
King crab
Weddell Seal
Antarctic Toothfish
Humpback whale
King penguin
Giant petrel
Southern elephant seal

Weddell Seals
Lantern fish
Snowy sheathbill
Antarctic fur seal
Chinstrap penguin
Sea stars
Antarctic springtail
Orca whale
Humboldt penguins
Short-tailed Shearwater
Wandering albatros
Trumpetfish
Crabeater seal
Sperm whale
Imperial shag
Ocellated icefish
Leopard seal

In the snow

Brrrr! It's cold at the poles, so don't hang around! How quickly can you speed through these chilly puzzles?

Maze

The reindeer are lost. Help them to find their way back to the herd.

CUTE CUBS

A polar bear mom almost always gives birth to two babies. The cubs live with their mom for up to three years.

Dot to dot

Connect the dots, starting at the number 1. Who will you find?

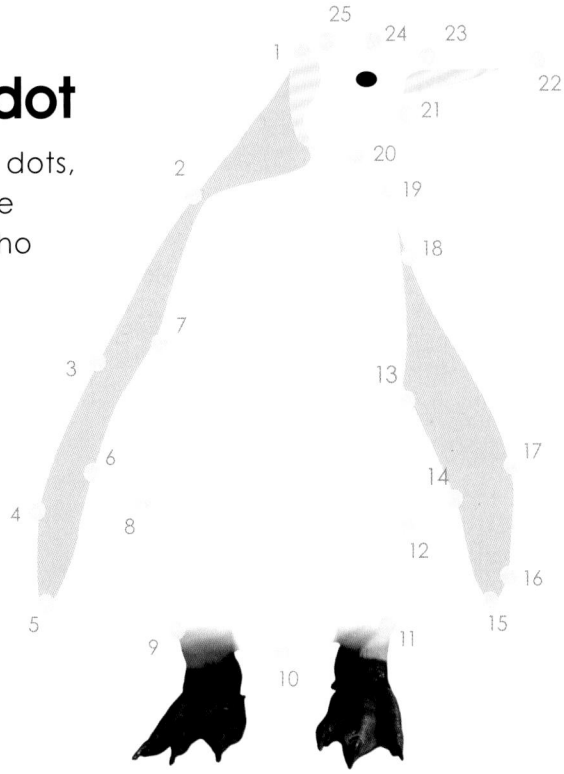

Odd one out

Look carefully at the penguin chicks. Which one doesn't match the others?

What comes next

Can you work out which polar animal comes next on each line?

Desert

Rolling seas of sand, or vast, rocky wastes, deserts are one of the world's most hostile habitats. Temperatures can range from baking hot during the day, to freezing cold at night, and sometimes no rain falls for years and years. It seems remarkable that animals can live in such inhospitable places, but they have many features to help them keep cool and find enough water. Some, like camels, can go for days without drinking. Others, like gerbils, shelter from the daytime heat in cool burrows underground.

Sidewinder
Scarab beetle
Fennec fox
Gila monster
Gemsbok
Vinegaroon
Spotted hyena
Bactrian camel
Armadillo
Crab spider
Centipede
Bearded dragon
Tarantula
Blister beetle
Ball python
Greater earless lizard
Darkling beetle
Pronghorn
Elf owl
Black-tailed jackrabbit
Baboon
Gerbil

California kingsnake
Ants
Rock hyrax
Desert iguana
Scorpion
Desert horned lizard
Ostrich
Sonoran desert toad
Black widow spider
Lappet-faced vulture
African wild dog cubs
Addax
Gray's monitor
Western scrub jay
Locust
Jerusalem cricket
Rosy boa
Bat
Great roadrunner

Hummingbird
Ringtail
Ankole longhorn cattle
Dingo
Sun spider
Caracal
Indian wild asses
Checkered beetle
African pygmy hedgehog
Aardvark
Thorny devil
Coyote
Longhorn beetle
Spadefoot toad
Chinkara/Indian gazelle
Chuckwalla
Damselfly
Desert tortoise
Burrowing owl
Desert bighorn sheep

Dromedary camel
Praying mantis
Bilby
Arabian oryx
Kangaroo rat
Australian spider beetle
African crested porcupine
Cicada
Rattlesnake
Armadillo lizard
Assassin bug
Cactus wren
Gila woodpecker
Black-footed cat
Burchells sandgrouse
Meerkat
Honeybee

In the desert

Phew, it's hot in the desert! Solve these puzzles and discover which animals live in the heat.

Matching pairs

Pair up these desert lizards. Which one does not have a matching twin?

SUNBATHERS

Meerkats live in tunnels that they dig under the desert sand. In the mornings they climb out to sunbathe and warm up.

Help the camel

The camel is trying to find the water hole. Which line should it take?

Word search

Can you find the desert animals in the word grid?

p	o	w	l	g
s	n	a	k	e
t	m	n	j	c
w	a	t	l	k
f	o	x	r	o

Gecko

Ant

Owl

Fox

Snake

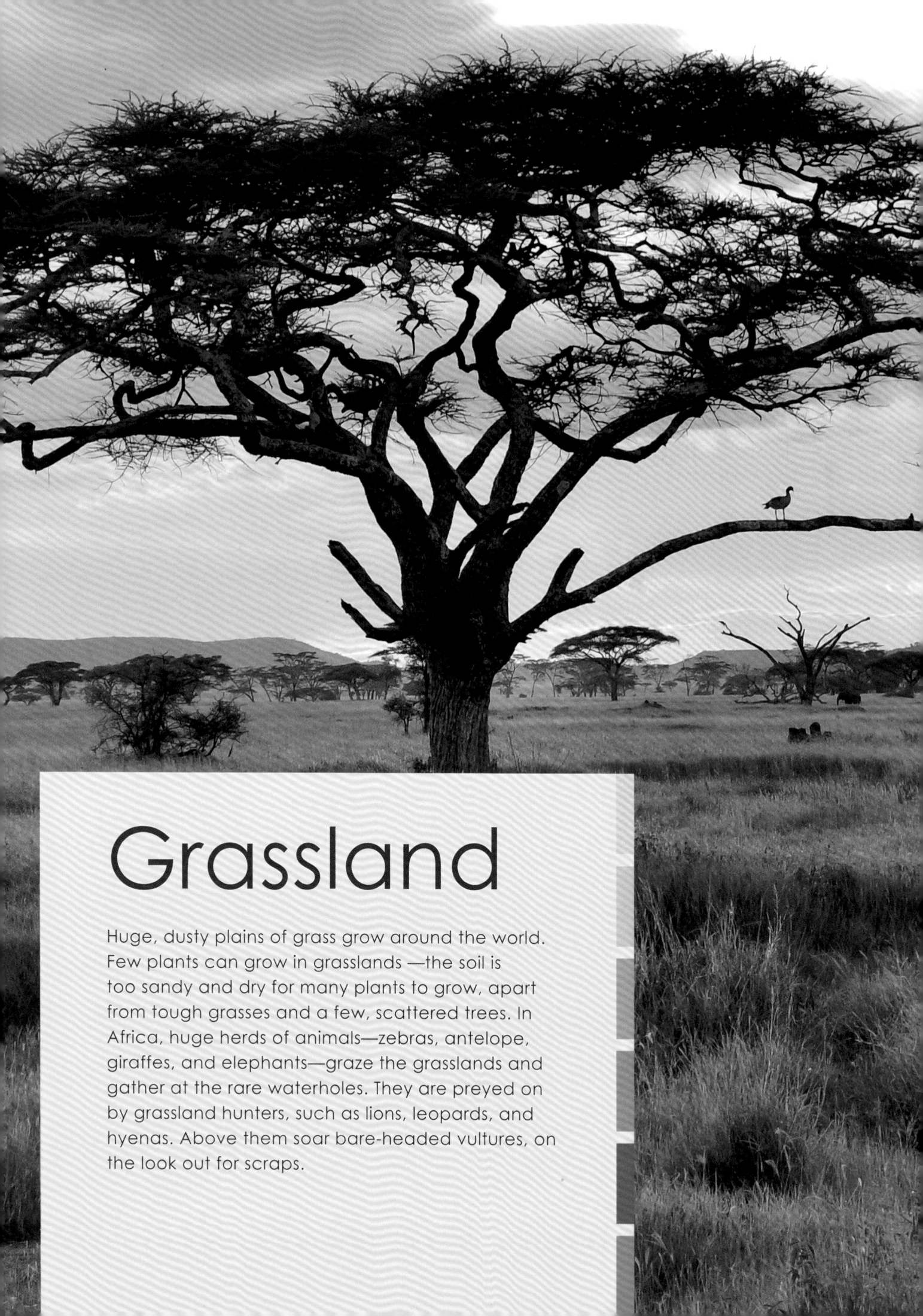

Grassland

Huge, dusty plains of grass grow around the world. Few plants can grow in grasslands —the soil is too sandy and dry for many plants to grow, apart from tough grasses and a few, scattered trees. In Africa, huge herds of animals—zebras, antelope, giraffes, and elephants—graze the grasslands and gather at the rare waterholes. They are preyed on by grassland hunters, such as lions, leopards, and hyenas. Above them soar bare-headed vultures, on the look out for scraps.

Wall brown butterfly
Leopard tortoise
Ants
Zebra
Meerkat
Jaguar
Helmeted guineafowl
Grasshopper
Dung beetle
Ferret
Cheetah
Egyptian cobra
Komodo dragon
White-backed vulture
Giant anteater
Termites
Hyena
Lion
Common blue butterfly
Lion cub
Caracal
Hoopoe
Dhole

Serval
Springbok
Skipper butterfly
Puff adder
African elephant
Grey crowned crane
Gaur
Black-backed jackel
Bush dog
Chameleon
Mole
Klipspinger
Hartebeest
Joey
Red kangaroo
Weaver bird
Barn owl
Pheasant
Locust
Leopard gecko

Ball Python
Ostrich
Impala
Thomson's gazelle
Red-tailed hawk
American bison
Black mamba
Grasshopper sparrow
Vervet monkey
Horse
Aardvark
Baboon spider
Nyala
Prairie dog
Vulturine guineafowl
Leopard
Egyptian vulture

Bumblebee
Wildebeest
Giraffe
Warthog
Mosquito
Griffon vulture
Greater kudu
Opossum
Black rhinoceros
Ticks
Firefly
Guanaco
Tiger
Ants
White rhinoceros
White lion
Emu
Fox
Buffalo
Simien wolf

On safari

It's time to head out into the grassland to spot some of the biggest, tallest, and fastest animals on Earth!

Sticker scene

Can you find the elephants on your sticker sheet? Add them to the grassland scene.

Use your stickers here!

SPEEDY CAT

The cheetah is the fastest running land animal in the world. It can run at full speed for about a minute.

How many left?

Count the nests and the birds. Are there enough nests for each weaver bird?

Find the shadows

Look at the shapes carefully. Can you match the animals to their shadows?

Can you find?

Look at the grassland animals. Can you find four tortoises, three butterflies, two birds, and one snake?

PRIDE OF LIONS

Lions live in families called prides. You can spot a male lion because it has a furry mane around its head.

Matching pair

Can you find two antelopes that are exactly the same?

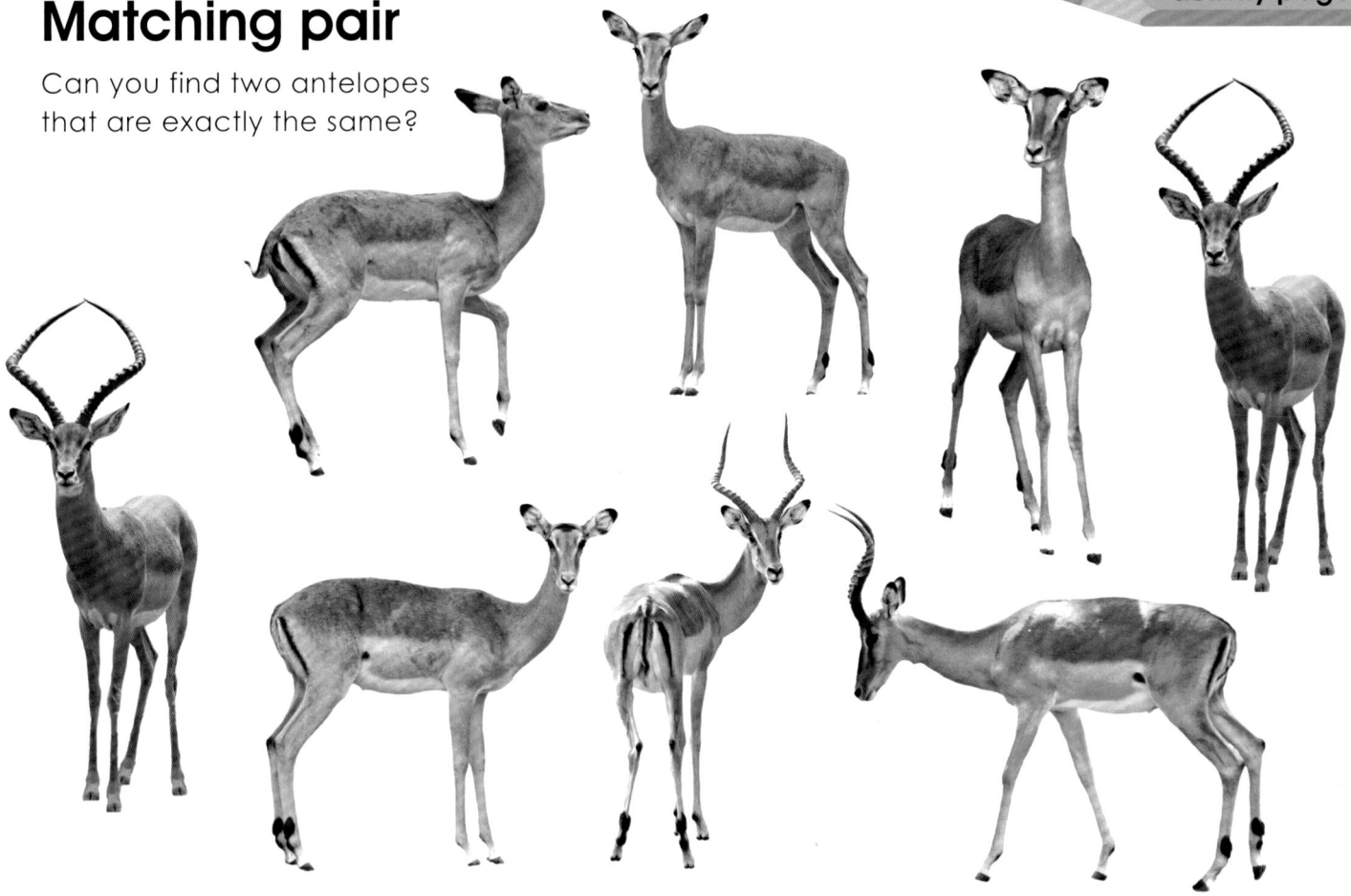

Color me in

Which colors will you choose for these dung beetles? Make them nice and bright!

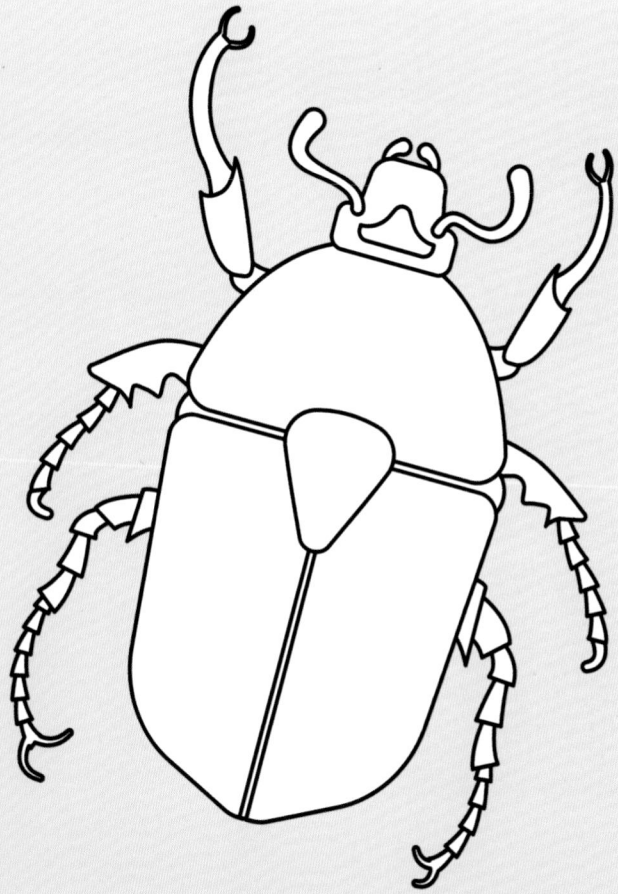

Rivers and Lakes

Starting off as a stream high up on a mountainside, a river flows downhill, fast at first, then slowing down as it reaches the sea, and its journey ends. On its way, it wears away waterfalls, scrapes away valleys, and fills lakes. Animals swim and feed underwater, or shelter in the plants that grow along the river bank. Many animals spend part of their lives in water, and part on land. Lakes are also home to hundreds of animals, including huge flocks of brightly-colored flamingoes on some African lakes.

Hippopotamus
Blue-spotted salamander
Fish eagle
Snake-head fish
Penguin tetra
Green anaconda
River crab
Coypu
Axolotl
Flamingos
Trout
Mandarin duck
Red discus fish
Stork
Blue discus fish
Black-crowned night heron
Dragonfly larvae

Amazon river dolphin
Fish eggs
Piranha
Leech
Fishing spider
Crocodile
Beaver
Scarlet ibis
Mayfly
Water snake
American Bullfrog
Crayfish
Walleye
Dalmatian pelican
Southern leopard frog
Alligator snapping turtle
Red lechwe
Otter
Pike
Water beetle
Coot
Monarch butterflies
Fishing owl
Giant snakehead fish
Carp

Albino American alligator
Stickleback
Fire Salamander
Damselfly
Salmon
Betta
Tadpole
Mosquito
Mallard duck
Duck-billed platypus
Eel
Barbel
Oscar fish
Waterbuck
Zooplankton
Kingfisher
Spoonbill
Alpine newt
Neon tetra
Black swan
Egret
Baikal seal
Koi carp
Red-eared slider

Ducklings
Manatee
Backswimmer
River snail
Catfish
Hydra
Sturgeon
Osprey
River dolphin
Water shrew
Toad
Freshwater prawn
Vole
River mussels
Pike perch
Water scorpion
Yellow perch
White swan
Alligator
Canada Goose
Lapwing
Clown featherback
European cormorant
Loon
African jewelfish

Down the river

Jump into a boat and take a trip down the river. Solve these puzzles to find out what lives under the moving water.

Dot to dot

Connect the dots, starting with the number 1. What's on the lily pad?

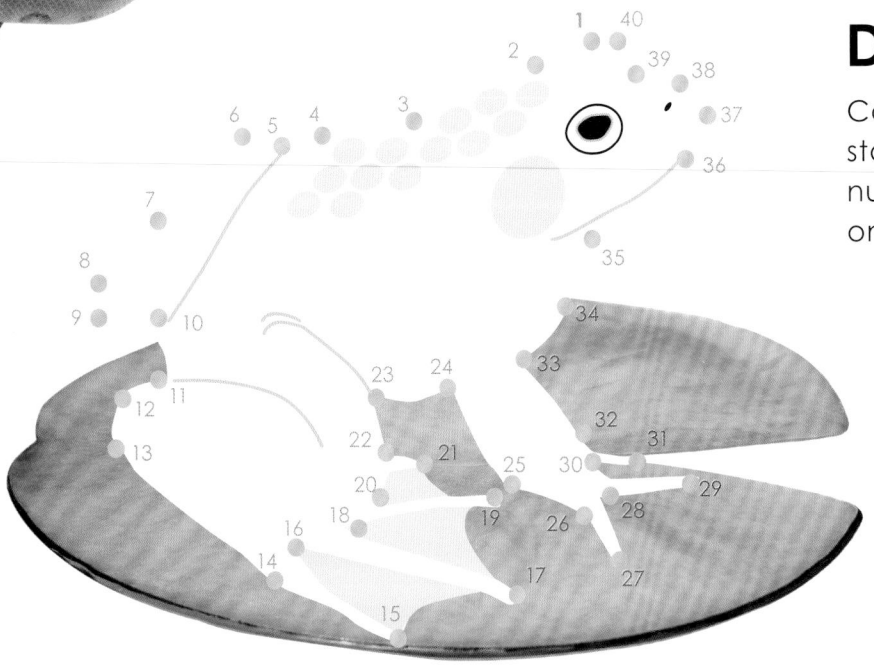

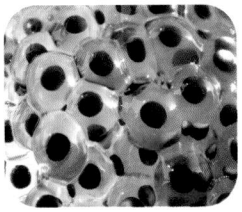

Matching pair

Look at the turtles. Can you find the matching pair?

PINK DOLPHIN

Most dolphins live in the ocean, but not this one! The pink river dolphin lives in the Amazon River.

Shadow search

Can you match the river animals to their shadows?

Maze

The kingfisher wants to dive for fish. Can you help it find its way to the river?

On the lake

There are lots of animals to spot on a lake. But keep watch! The lake may look calm, but danger lurks beneath.

Follow the lines

The otters are hunting for the crayfish. Which one will find it?

SNAP!

Watch out for the Nile crocodile as it hunts in the lake. All you can see is its eyes, ears, and nostrils above the water.

Matching pair

Look at the long-legged flamingos. Can you find the matching pair?

What comes next?

Look at the animal patterns. Can you work out which lake animal comes next on each line?

Use your stickers here!

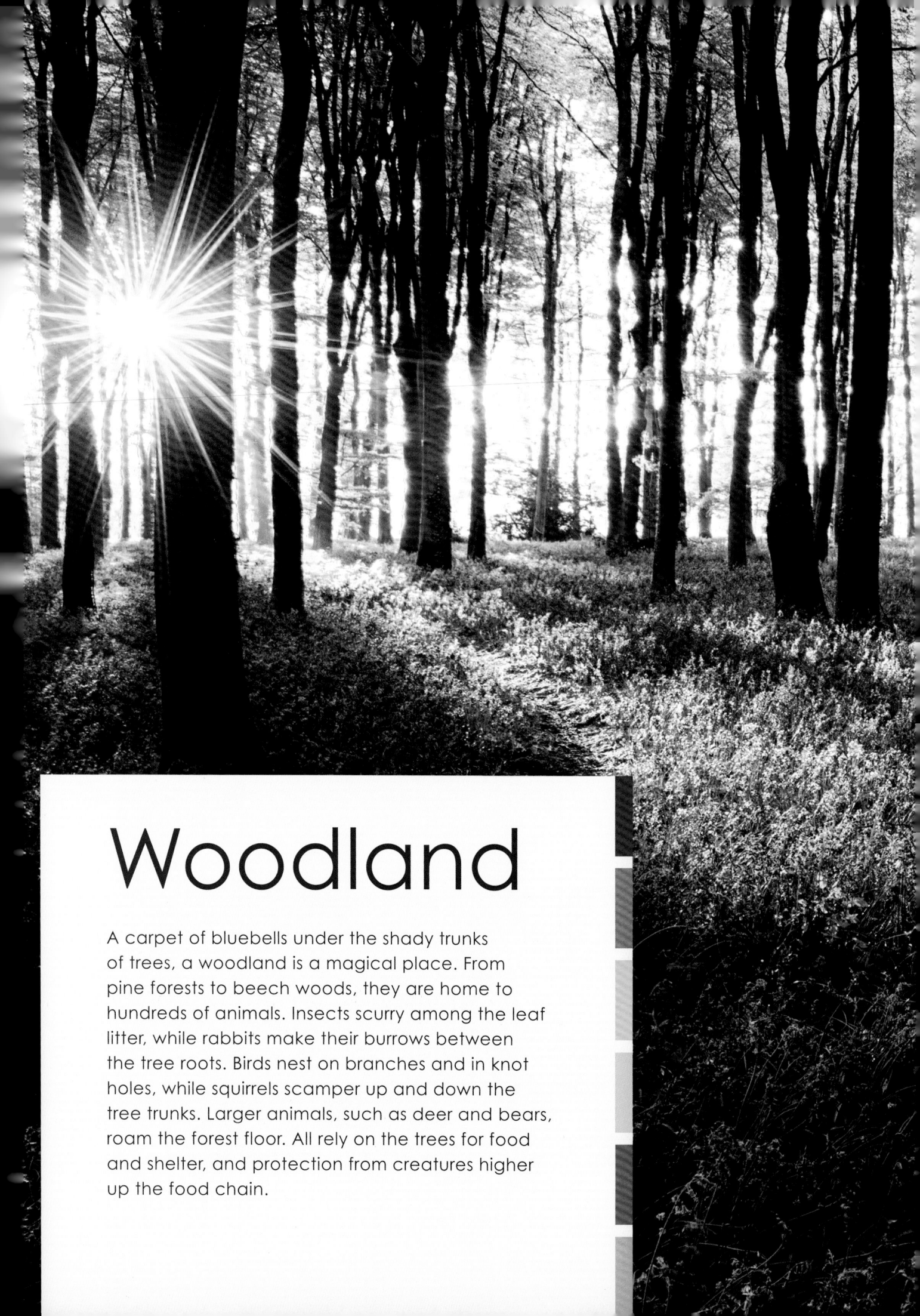

Woodland

A carpet of bluebells under the shady trunks of trees, a woodland is a magical place. From pine forests to beech woods, they are home to hundreds of animals. Insects scurry among the leaf litter, while rabbits make their burrows between the tree roots. Birds nest on branches and in knot holes, while squirrels scamper up and down the tree trunks. Larger animals, such as deer and bears, roam the forest floor. All rely on the trees for food and shelter, and protection from creatures higher up the food chain.

Fire salamander
Brimstone butterfly
Smooth snake
Ferret
Crowned sifaka
Brown bear
Termite
Wolf spider
Blue tit
Slow worm
Lemur
Long-eared owl
Comma butterfly
Kudu
Hedgehog
Tasmanian devil
Sika deer
Porcupine
Honeybees
Black bear
Banana slug
Bumblebee

Horsefly
Beaver
White rhinoceros
Tree frog
Corn snake
Bat
Adder
Moose
Wood ants
Hairstreak butterfly
Map butterfly
Red squirrel
Woodboring beetles
Turtle dove
Common lizard
Wolverine
Wood pigeon
Eagle owl
Ticks
Green tiger beetle
Earthworm
White admiral butterfly
Deer
Ermine
Ladybird
Racoon

Red-bellied wood-pecker
Goat moth
Woodlouse
Orb weaver spider
Fox
Reindeer
Striped skunk
Woodlouse spider
Garden spider
Grey squirrel
Purple emporor
Bee eater
Gatekeeper butterfly
Burnet moth
Mole
Grass snake
Barbary ground squirrel
Cardinal beetle
Kookaburra
Silver-washed fritillary
Badger
Elk
Wild boar
Death watch beetle
Caterpillar

Orange tip butterfly
Wasp
Caribou
Gypsy moth
Tamarin
Mink
Opossum
Chipmunk
Speckled wood butterfly
Baboon
Hummingbird
Peacock butterfly
Black grouse
Crab spider
Longhorn beetle
Soldier beetle
Koala
Dragonfly
Wolf
Pine marten
Ringlet butterflies
Devil's coach horse beetle

In the woods

Shhh. Woodland creatures are shy. Try to keep quiet while you work through these puzzles.

Sticker scene

Can you find the flying owls on your sticker sheet? Add them to the woodland scene.

Use your stickers here!

A PANDA'S LIFE

Pandas live in bamboo forests and love to eat bamboo. In fact, bamboo is about the only thing the pandas eat. They eat it all day!

Odd one out

Look carefully at the skunks. Which one doesn't match the others?

Word search

Can you find the woodland creatures in the word grid?

p	m	s	t	m
b	o	a	r	o
a	l	h	n	t
t	e	i	x	h
m	d	e	e	r

Bat

Moth

Boar

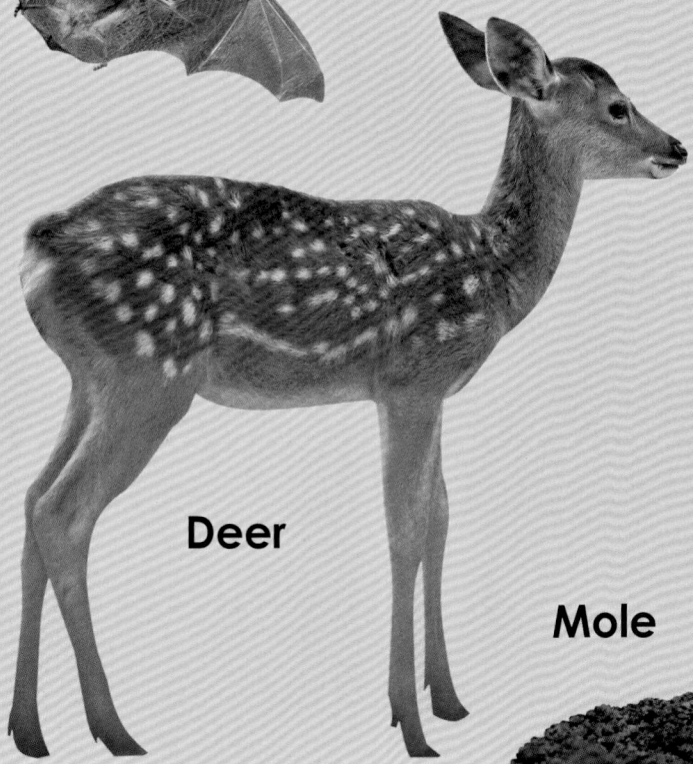

Deer

Mole

Reefs

Like a beautiful underwater garden, a coral reef is a stunning habitat that bursts with color and life. Fish in coats of vibrant colors dart between corals in the shape of antlers, daisies, mushrooms, and even brains. They swim in large shoals for safety. Octopuses and sea snakes hide in nooks and crannies, while giant, blue-lipped clams sit on the sea floor. Reefs are rich feeding grounds for lurking reef sharks, and rare sea turtles. And, once the daytime creatures go to sleep, a community of night-time animals take over.

Lyretail hogfish
Knifefish
Lion's mane jellyfish
Black pomfret
Spiny dogfish
Butterfish
Purple Anthias
Talang queenfish
Blackside hawkfish
Leopard shark
Grey reef shark
Bengal sergeant
Clownfish
Leopard coral grouper
Mahi mahi
Bottlenose dolphins
Mandarin fish
Brain coral
Shrimp
Kuhl's maskray
Sea urchin
Suckerfish
Flatworm
Frogfish
Blenny

Red sea bream
Flounder
Giant barrel sponge
Striped eel catfish
Hawksbill turtle
Blue-ringed octopus
Small-spotted catshark
Grouper fish
Sea slug
Purple tang
Goatfish
Coral
Pygmy seahorse
Toadfish
Large-toothed cardinalfish
Sprat fish
Unicornfish
Sea slug
Long-spine porcupinefish
Rabbitfish
Maldivian Lyretail
Demoiselle
Staghorn coral
Purple firefish
Saddleback clownfish
Angelfish
Whale shark

Blue-spotted stingray
Anenome
Butterflyfish
Crown of thorns starfish
Yellowtail fusilier
Hermit crab
Perch
Squirrelfish
Soldierfish
Longfin spotted snake-eel
Sea cucumbers
Scorpionfish
Pipefish
Barracuda
Parrot fish
Jewel fairy basslet
Coralfish
Sea anenome
Sea goldie
Silver biddy
Spotted sweetlips
Barred soapfish
Seahorse
Yellowtail scad
Banggai cardinalfish
Reef octopus
Grunter fish
Spider crab
Coral polyps

Pigfish
Diamond trevally
Coral hind
Seaperch
Sea anemone
Trumpetfish
Zebra cling fish
Batfish
Butterfly fish
Banded sea krait
Striped surgeonfish
Mangrove red snapper
Harlequin sweetlips
Moray eel
Stonefish
Tripletail
Garfish
Razorfish
Clown triggerfish
Murena spotted eel
Lionfish
Giant clam
Wrasse
Bannerfish
Red gurnard
Redfin velvetfish

On the reef

The coral reef is very colorful. Look at all the spotted, striped, multi-colored sea creatures. But watch out for the hungry shark!

Matching pair

Look at the reef fish. Can you spot two that are exactly the same?

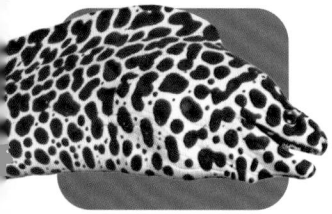

CORAL HOME

Coral reefs are home to many sea creatures. In fact a quarter of all types of sea creatures live on or around the reefs!

Color me in

Use blues, greens, and yellows to brighten up this octopus.

Spot the difference

Can you find two differences between these sea slugs?

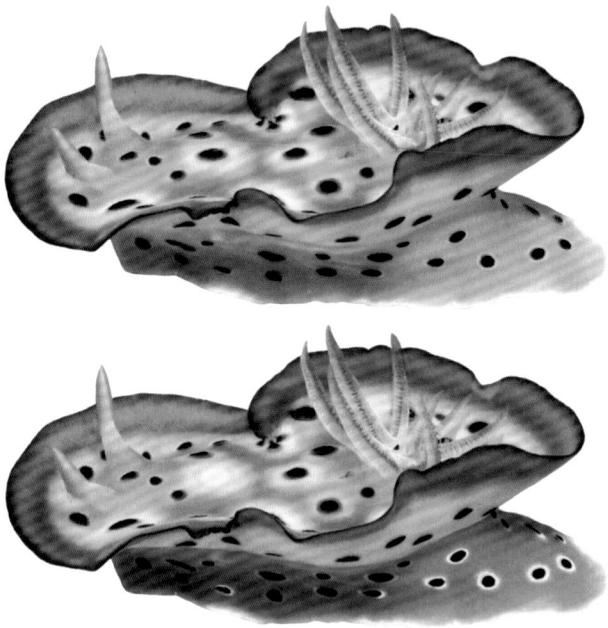

Maze

The clown fish is searching for somewhere to hide. Help it reach the anemone.

start

finish

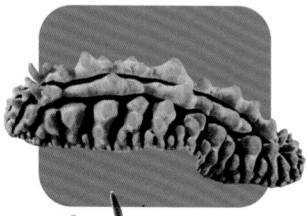

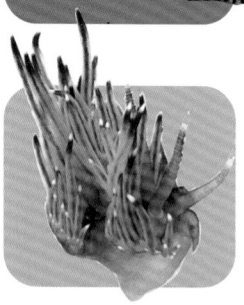

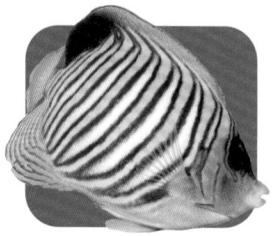

Which way home?

The parrot fish wants to find its way home to the reef. Which line should it take?

Draw the other half

Can you draw the other half of the jellyfish?

DON'T EAT ME!

The lionfish is very beautiful but very dangerous. It has poisonous and deadly spines. Other fish don't try to eat it!

Count the legs

Count the arms and legs. Which reef animal has the most?

Shadow match

The reef shark is hunting. Match the shadow to see which sea creature it is chasing.

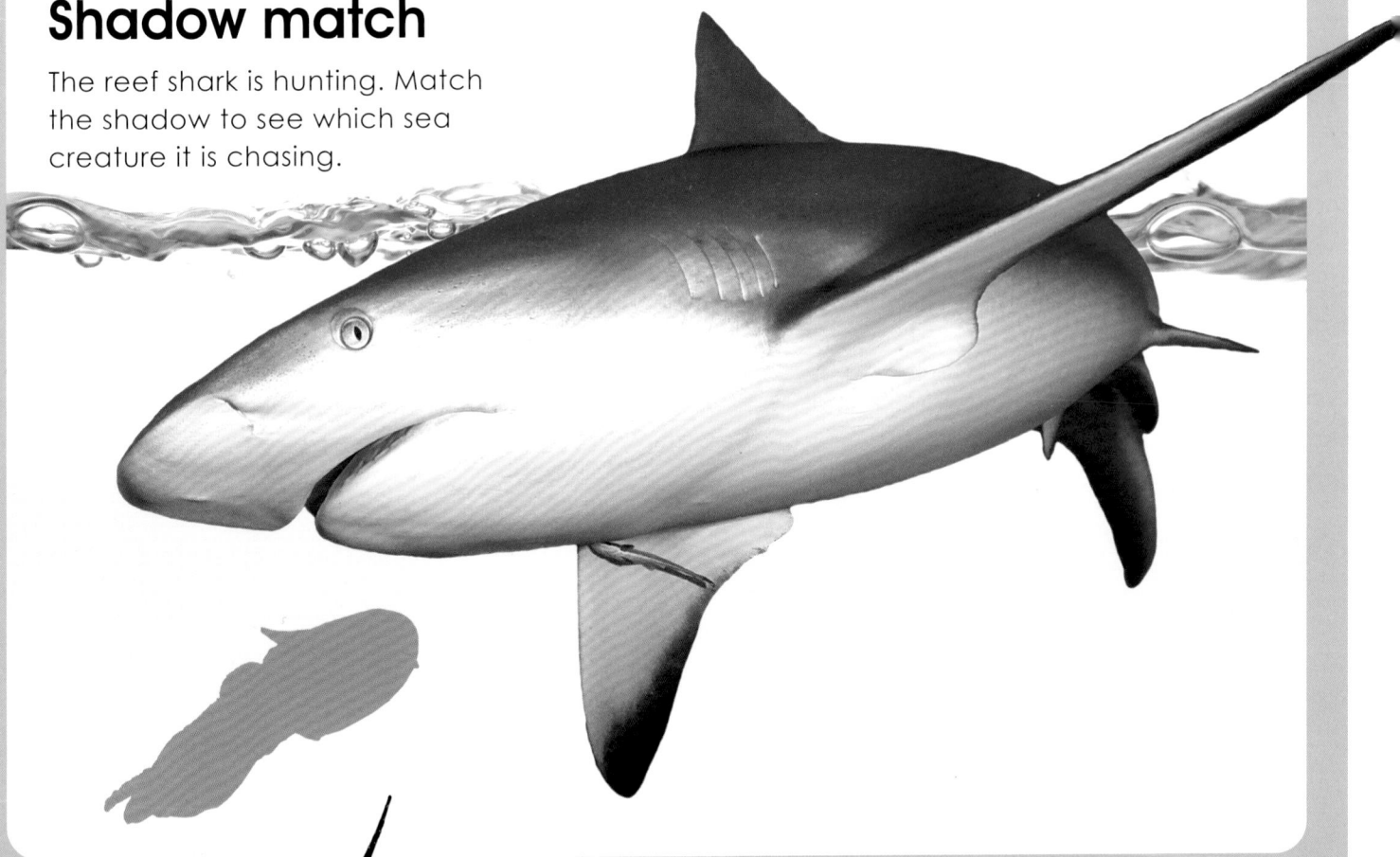

Stingray Starfish Squid Turtle

Urban

The hustle and bustle of a city might seem an unlikely place to find animals. But parks, gardens, and city buildings have become a valuable habitat for wildlife. Many animals move to the city because their natural habitat is under threat. The city offers them plenty of places to shelter, and rich pickings of food, often from trash cans and garbage. Animals quickly adapt to their new surroundings. Instead of trees, birds nest in chimneys and roof eaves, or in nesting boxes in people's gardens.

Rabbit
Python
Mosquito
Rooster
Hamster
Ferret
Mallard duck
Red squirrel
Cockatoo
Chicks
Moth
Pigeon
Lizard
Zebra angelfish
Sphynx cat
Tarantula
Labrador retriever puppy
African grey parrot
Koi fish
French bulldog
Weimaraner
Seagull

Ladybug
Parakeet
Goat
Butterflies
Shrew
Sheep
Scorpion
Cat
Bats
Crow
Racoon
Ducklings
Chow chow
Locust
Garden snail
Fox
Telescope goldfish
Skunk
Lovebirds
Chicken
Mallard duck
Termites
Bumblebee
Toad

Piglets
Goldfish
Quails
Chipmunk
Cockroach
Corn snake
Housefly
Peacock
Gecko
Iguana
Guinea pig
Mute swan
Green turtle
Silkworm
Parrot
Gerbil
Ants
Owl
Rats
Turkey
Gray squirrel
English bulldog
Brahman calf
Dalmatian puppy
Mouse

House spider
Hedgehog
Red setter
Aphids
Maltese
Flea
Hare
Slug
Wasp
Pony
Cricket
Siamese cat
Dove
Chicken
Garden spider
Common lizard
Earthworm
Grasshopper
Ticks
Common kestrel
Goose
Siberian husky puppy
Canary
Cow
Honeybee
Tortoise
House moth

In the city

Step into the city to see all sorts of pets and wild animals. There are more animals living with us than you might think!

Follow the lines

Follow the lines to help the animals find their babies.

CITY SINGERS

City foxes live in family groups. They can jump over high garden fences and often make their dens in garden sheds.

Matching pair

Look at the six kittens. Can you find the matching pair?

Word search

Find the town animals in the word grid.

p	d	t	c	b
m	o	u	s	e
h	g	w	l	e
c	a	t	r	u
k	d	o	v	e

Bee

Dog

Cat

Dove

Mouse

Camouflage

Now you see it. Now you don't. Some animals have adapted to their habitats in clever ways. They have special colors or patterns to help them blend into their surroundings, so that they stay safe from hungry predators. In the rainforest, some animals, such as insects, are disguised as the leaves they feed on. In the deserts, some lizards match the stony ground. Some animals, such as this snake, use their cunning camouflage to sneak up on their prey without being seen. Its unfortunate victim will not spot it, until it's too late.

Leaf insects/
katydids
Python
Owl butterfly
Stick insects
Spiny leaf
insect
Lappet
moth
Leafwing
butterfly
Pine
beetle
Gelatin slug
caterpillar
Fer-de-lance
Stonefish
Merveille
du Jour moth
Gecko
Slow
worm
Praying mantis
Luna
moth
Deer
Birdwing
butterflies
Annam
spadefoot
toad
Baby
harp
seal
Green parrot
Owlet
moth
Golden
orb
spider
African bullfrog
Rock
hyrax

Chameleon
Ticks
Earthworm
Arctic fox
Locust
Lynx
Orchid mantis
Lunar thorn moth
Ball python
Rhino beetle
Snowy sheathbill
Puff adder
Koala
Fox
Lion
Leopard
Lime hawk moth
Gray tree frog
Anole
Caterpillar
Woodcock

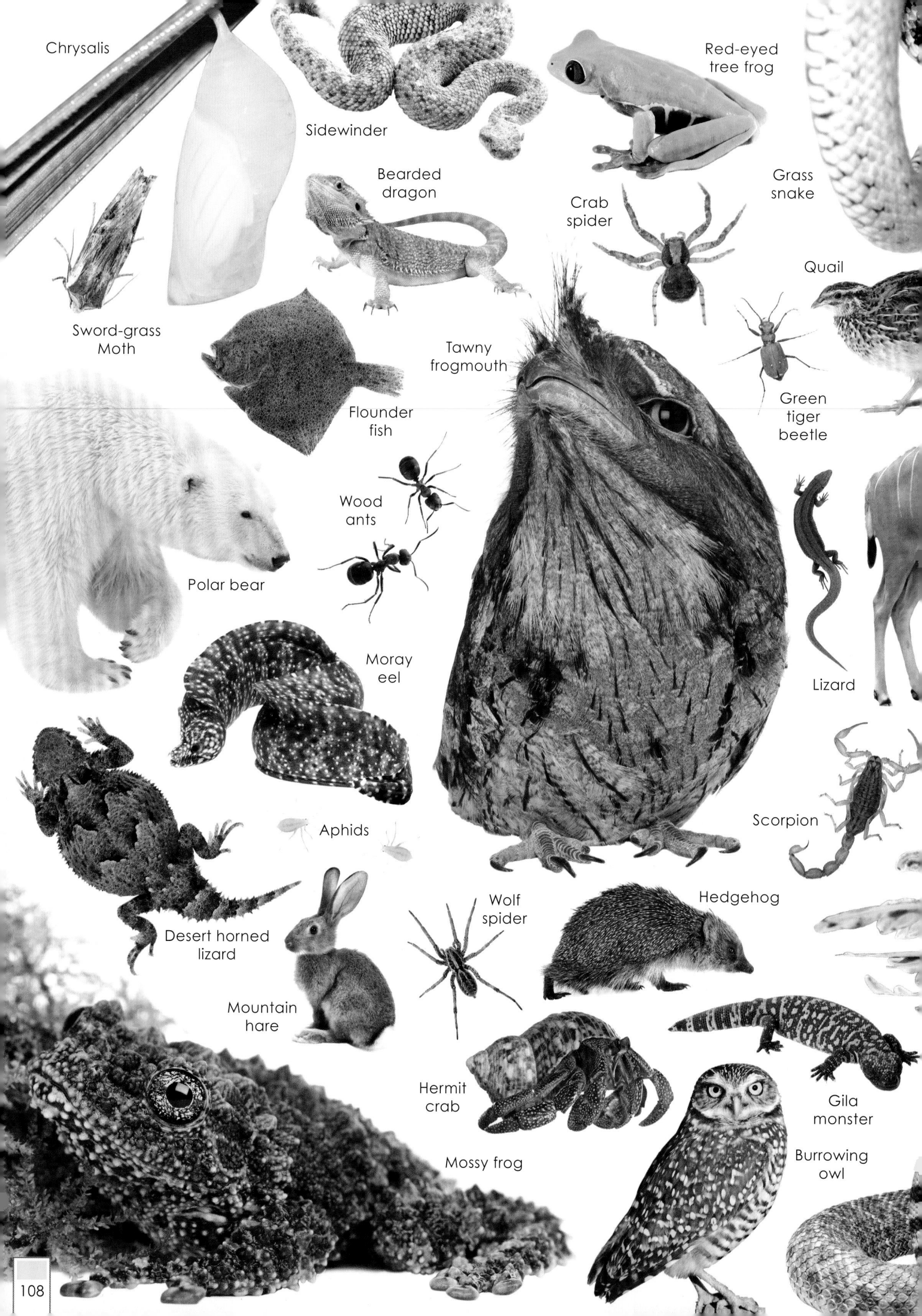
Chrysalis
Sidewinder
Red-eyed tree frog
Grass snake
Bearded dragon
Crab spider
Quail
Sword-grass Moth
Tawny frogmouth
Green tiger beetle
Flounder fish
Wood ants
Polar bear
Lizard
Moray eel
Scorpion
Aphids
Hedgehog
Wolf spider
Desert horned lizard
Mountain hare
Hermit crab
Gila monster
Mossy frog
Burrowing owl

Green lacewing
Garden snail
Woolly bear caterpillar
Cuttlefish
Leaf-tailed gecko
Kudu
Red squirrel
Leafhopper Larva
Green tree python
Cheetah
Barnacles
Grasshopper
Spider
Porcupine
Giant peacock moth
Toad
Leafy sea dragon
Stink bug
Dock bug
Scorpion fish
Iguana
Rattlesnake
Reef octopus

Camouflage

You'll have to look carefully to solve these puzzles. These animals know how to hide!

Maze

The bush cricket is trying to reach the leaves. Can you help it reach them?

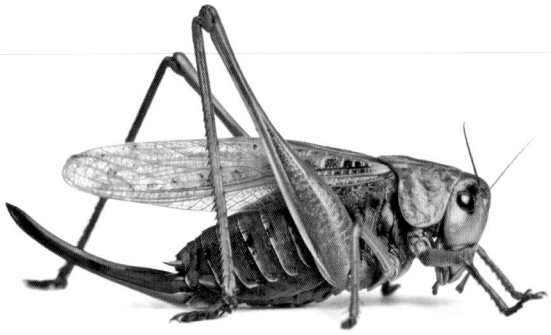

start

finish

HIDE AND SEEK

Even a big animal can hide against its background. This giraffe is the same color as the grassland and can be difficult to spot.

Can you find?

Each animal is hiding in the picture below it. Can you spot each one?

Snake

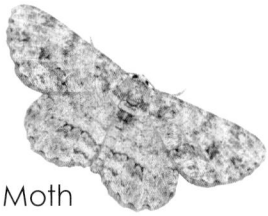

Moth

Stick insect

Frog

Jaguar

Sticker scene

Look on your sticker sheet. Can you find any animals that could hide in this scene?

Use your stickers here!